This is Dot.

Dot has a pot.

The pot has a top.

"What is in the pot, Dot?"

"A lot," said Dot.

"A rock and a sock...

a box and a fox,

a dog and a frog,

a lock and a clock!"

"Stop!" said Pop.

"It is hot in the pot!"

With a hop...

and a flop,

and a plop,...

all got out of the pot.

Dot got a mop!